Would you rather?
Eww
EDITION
for kids

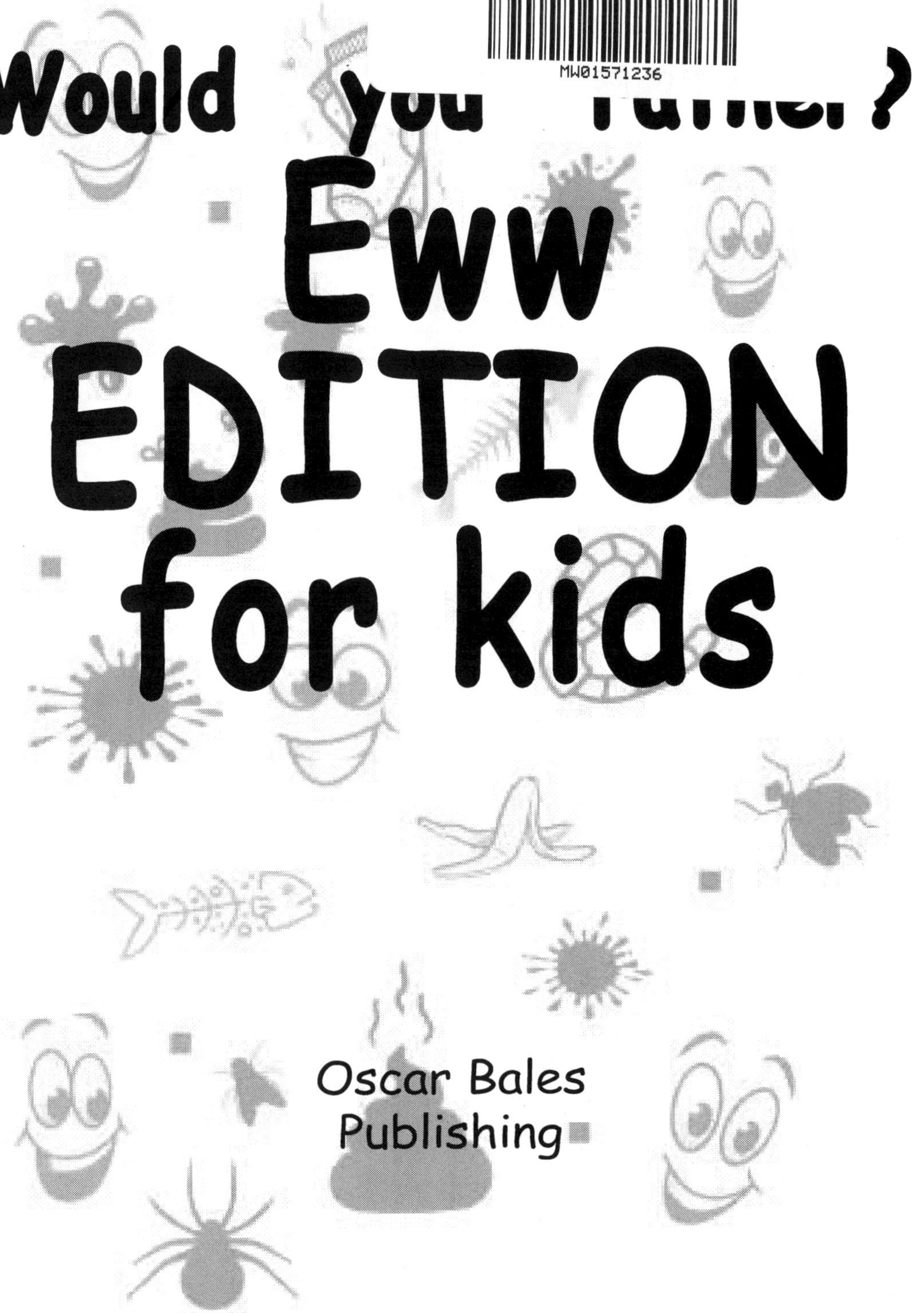

Oscar Bales
Publishing

© Copyright 2021 - All rights reserved.

The content contained within this book may not be reproduced, duplicated or transmitted without direct written permission from the author
 or the publisher. Under no circumstances will any blame or legal responsibility be held against the publisher, or author, for any damages, reparation, or monetary loss due to the information contained within this book. Either directly or indirectly.
Legal Notice:
This book is copyright protected. This book is only for personal use. You cannot amend, distribute, sell, use, quote or paraphrase any part, or the content within this book, without the consent of the author or publisher.
Disclaimer Notice:
Please note the information contained within this document is for educational and entertainment purposes only. All effort has been executed to present accurate, up to date, and reliable, complete information. No warranties of any kind are declared or implied.
Readers acknowledge that the author is not engaging in the rendering of legal, financial, medical or professional advice. The content within this book has been derived from various sources. Please consult a licensed professional before attempting any techniques outlined in this book.
By reading this document, the reader agrees that under no circumstances is the author responsible for any losses, direct or indirect, which are incurred as a result of the use of information contained within this document, including, but not limited to, — errors, omissions, or inaccuracies.

STOP! Don't move forward without...
YOUR FREE GIFT

1# BUNUS - Travel Jokes [PDF]

» The ultimate **40 TRAVEL JOKES** to convert any boring, long road trip and more into fun, education, and unforgettable moments with the family or friends!

» The **25th** will amaze the whole family and laugh endlessly

2# BUNUS - Special Funny Video [10 min]

» This video is safe and can really bring tons of laughter to your kids' day, also useful to reduce stress, eases anxiety and tension!

» Watch the videos with your kids is also a great way to build fun memories and to strengthen the bonds of relationship with them

» In minute **3:40** you will laugh so much that you will tear on the ground

SCAN ME **NOW** to get Your FREE GIFT - - - →

or go to
www.subscribepage.com/wouldyourather

Welcome to
WOULD YOU RATHER?
EWW EDITION
for KIDS

RULES :

* Face your opponent and decide who is 'Player 1' and 'Player 2'.

* Starting with 'Player 1', read the Would You Rather question aloud and pick an answer. The same player will then explain why they chose that answer in the most hilarious or wacky way possible!

* If the reason makes 'Player 2' laugh, then a laugh point is scored!

* Take turns going back and forth, then mark your total laugh points at the end of each round!

* Whoever gets the most laugh points is officially crowned the 'Laugh Champion'!

* If ending with a tie, finish with the Tie-Breaker round for WINNER TAKES ALL

Most importantly have fun and be SILLY
REMEMBER these scenarios listed in
the book are solely for fun and games!
Please do NOT attempt any of the
crazy scenarios in the book

Player 1

(DON'T FORGET TO EXPLAIN YOUR ANSWERS!)

Would you rather eat feces from your school toilet for a month OR defecate and sleep in your room for a month?

/1
Laugh Point

Would you rather fart every time you laugh or burp every time you cry?

/1
Laugh Point

Player 1

(DON'T FORGET TO EXPLAIN YOUR ANSWERS!)

Would you rather sleep in the garbage truck for a week or sleep in a septic tank for a week?

/1
Laugh Point

Would you rather have a frog for a pet or a rat for a pet?

/1
Laugh Point

Pass the book to Player 2 !... →

Player 2

(DON'T FORGET TO EXPLAIN YOUR ANSWERS!)

Would you rather eat raw meat or spoiled food?

/1
Laugh Point

Would you rather cough up hairballs like a cat or slobber like a dog?

/1
Laugh Point

Player 2

(DON'T FORGET TO EXPLAIN YOUR ANSWERS!)

Would you rather be stuck in an elevator with a skunk or a car with a stinky pig?

/1
Laugh Point

Would you rather have teeth for a tongue or hair for lips

/1
Laugh Point

Player 1 /4
ROUD TOTAL

Player 2 /4
ROUD TOTAL

ROUD WINNER

Player

(DON'T FORGET TO EXPLAIN YOUR ANSWERS!)

Would you be Jacob sartorius's stinky shoe or Jojo Siwa's toothbrush?

/1
Laugh Point

Would you rather have all your fingers stuck together with thread or have bunions on your shoulders?

/1
Laugh Point

Player

(DON'T FORGET TO EXPLAIN YOUR ANSWERS!)

Would you rather eat dog food or cat food?

/1
Laugh Point

Would you rather fight bats in space or wrestle a gorilla in the mud?

/1
Laugh Point

Pass the book to Player 2 !... →

Player 2

(DON'T FORGET TO EXPLAIN YOUR ANSWERS!)

Would you rather trip in the cafeteria every day or pee your pants in class for a week?

/1
Laugh Point

Would you rather drink sour milk straight from a cow or eat pizza out of the trash?

/1
Laugh Point

Player 2

(DON'T FORGET TO EXPLAIN YOUR ANSWERS!)

Would you rather have praying mantis eyes OR a spider's head?

/1
Laugh Point

Would you rather smell like rotten eggs or sour milk all the time?

/1
Laugh Point

Player 1 /4
ROUD TOTAL

Player 2 /4
ROUD TOTAL

ROUD WINNER

Player 1

(DON'T FORGET TO EXPLAIN YOUR ANSWERS!)

Would you rather sound like a cricket every time you move or croak every time you talk?

/1 Laugh Point

Would you rather eat sour patch kids off a cat litter box OR have used toothpaste ice-cream?

/1 Laugh Point

Player

(DON'T FORGET TO EXPLAIN YOUR ANSWERS!)

Would you rather look like a troll or have hard skin like an ogre?

/1
Laugh Point

Would you rather see only the color red or hear in whispers?

/1
Laugh Point

Pass the book to Player 2 !... →

Player 2

(DON'T FORGET TO EXPLAIN YOUR ANSWERS!)

Would you rather never have a life without air conditioning or never be able to use deodorant?

/1
Laugh Point

Would you rather infuriate mom or dad?

/1
Laugh Point

Player

(DON'T FORGET TO EXPLAIN YOUR ANSWERS!)

Would you rather have to shave your head or have your nose pierced?

/1
Laugh Point

Would you rather be extremely allergic to your favorite food or forced to eat your least favorite food once a week?

/1
Laugh Point

Player  /4
ROUD TOTAL

Player 2 /4
ROUD TOTAL

Player 1

(DON'T FORGET TO EXPLAIN YOUR ANSWERS!)

Would you rather have to make a one-minute speech in front of 10,000 people or have to kiss a frog

/1
Laugh Point

Would you rather only be able to get around by bouncing like a kangaroo or leaping like a ballerina?

/1
Laugh Point

Player

(DON'T FORGET TO EXPLAIN YOUR ANSWERS!)

Would you rather constantly worry about germs or be terrified of a monster under your bed?

___/1
Laugh Point

Would you rather never get tired or never have to go to the bathroom?

___/1
Laugh Point

Pass the book to Player 2 !... →

Player 2

(DON'T FORGET TO EXPLAIN YOUR ANSWERS!)

Would you rather be the ugliest person in the world or smell the worst?

/1
Laugh Point

Would you rather eyes all around your head or noses?

/1
Laugh Point

Player

(DON'T FORGET TO EXPLAIN YOUR ANSWERS!)

Would you rather always have lousy gas or always have a parched mouth?

/1
Laugh Point

Would you rather have to always hop around on one foot or have to always squat?

/1
Laugh Point

Player

ROUD TOTAL

Player

/4

ROUD TOTAL

ROUD WINNER

Player 1

(DON'T FORGET TO EXPLAIN YOUR ANSWERS!)

Would you rather have rainbows or flowers shoot out of your eyes?

/1
Laugh Point

Would you rather go a year with no eyelashes or go a year with no eyebrows?

/1
Laugh Point

Player 1

(DON'T FORGET TO EXPLAIN YOUR ANSWERS!)

Would you rather never be able to shower again or not be able to shave your legs?

/1
Laugh Point

Would you rather have a huge booger hanging out of your nose for the rest of your life or a pimple on your forehead for the rest of your life?

/1
Laugh Point

Pass the book to Player 2 !... →

Player 2

(DON'T FORGET TO EXPLAIN YOUR ANSWERS!)

Would you rather have webbed feet or webbed hands?

/1
Laugh Point

Would you rather dance like a monkey or dance like a bear?

/1
Laugh Point

Player 2

(DON'T FORGET TO EXPLAIN YOUR ANSWERS!)

Would you rather look like a skunk or smell like a skunk?

/1
Laugh Point

Would you rather lick a dirty trash can or moldy food?

/1
Laugh Point

Player  /4
ROUD TOTAL

Player 2 /4
ROUD TOTAL

ROUD WINNER

Player 1

(DON'T FORGET TO EXPLAIN YOUR ANSWERS!)

Would you rather only eat foods that look disgusting or smell disgusting?

/1 Laugh Point

Would you rather have to take one bite every day of the stinkiest cheese or a fresh snail from the ocean?

/1 Laugh Point

Player

(DON'T FORGET TO EXPLAIN YOUR ANSWERS!)

Would you rather sweat slime or honey?

/1
Laugh Point

Would you rather have a giant tongue or giant feet?

/1
Laugh Point

Pass the book to Player 2 !... →

Player 2

(DON'T FORGET TO EXPLAIN YOUR ANSWERS!)

Would you rather hold slugs or spiders in your hands?

/1
Laugh Point

Would you rather rub ketchup or mustard all over your body?

/1
Laugh Point

Player

(DON'T FORGET TO EXPLAIN YOUR ANSWERS!)

Would you rather burp up soap bubbles or worms?

/1
Laugh Point

Would you rather eat 5 boxes of Popeye's biscuit without any liquid to wash it down OR raw fish eyes with whipped cream topping?

/1
Laugh Point

Player 1   /4
ROUD TOTAL

Player 2   /4
ROUD TOTAL

ROUD WINNER

Player

(DON'T FORGET TO EXPLAIN YOUR ANSWERS!)

Would you rather jump into a vat of slime or a vat of sour milk?

/1
Laugh Point

Would you rather eat out of a bowl your dog has slobbered in OR eat a cake your cat has peed on?

/1
Laugh Point

Player

(DON'T FORGET TO EXPLAIN YOUR ANSWERS!)

Would you rather jump into a vat of slime or a vat of sour milk?

/1
Laugh Point

Would you rather roll in mud or a pile of ladybugs?

/1
Laugh Point

Pass the book to Player 2 !... →

Player 2

(DON'T FORGET TO EXPLAIN YOUR ANSWERS!)

Would you rather smell vomit or fart?

/1
Laugh Point

Would you rather swim in pudding or ice cream?

/1
Laugh Point

Player 2

(DON'T FORGET TO EXPLAIN YOUR ANSWERS!)

Would you rather be smacked in the face with a fish or farted on?

/1
Laugh Point

Would you rather be able to speak every language on earth or communicate with aliens?

/1
Laugh Point

Player 1 /4
ROUD TOTAL

Player 2 /4
ROUD TOTAL

ROUD WINNER

Player 1

(DON'T FORGET TO EXPLAIN YOUR ANSWERS!)

Would you rather get kissed by 100 people who haven't brushed for a year OR live in a house that hasn't been cleaned in 5 years?

/1
Laugh Point

Would you rather burp poop OR have little pieces of poop in your nose all the time?

/1
Laugh Point

Player

(DON'T FORGET TO EXPLAIN YOUR ANSWERS!)

Would you rather be able to understand what animals are saying or have the ability to be invisible?

/1
Laugh Point

Would you rather fight in a plant war as lettuce OR in a candy war as a potato-flavored gumdrop?

/1
Laugh Point

Pass the book to Player 2 !... →

Player 2

(DON'T FORGET TO EXPLAIN YOUR ANSWERS!)

Would you rather be able to fly like a bird or swim like a fish?

/1 Laugh Point

Would you rather be able to only lick food OR swallow it?

/1 Laugh Point

Player 2

(DON'T FORGET TO EXPLAIN YOUR ANSWERS!)

Would you rather lick the bottom of someone else's shoe or the sole of their feet?

/1
Laugh Point

Would you rather try to go to the washroom on a tiny toilet that will overflow or a giant toilet you might fall into?

/1
Laugh Point

Player 1 /4
ROUD TOTAL

Player 2 /4
ROUD TOTAL

ROUD WINNER

Player

(DON'T FORGET TO EXPLAIN YOUR ANSWERS!)

Would you rather have someone catch you picking your nose and eating it or scratching your bum and sniffing your fingers?

/1
Laugh Point

Would you rather scrub the washroom floor with your toothbrush and then use it to clean your teeth, or clean your teeth with a toothbrush someone else has used in their mouth?

/1
Laugh Point

Player

(DON'T FORGET TO EXPLAIN YOUR ANSWERS!)

Would you rather have beetles in your hair for a week or in your food for a day?

/1
Laugh Point

Would you rather scrub the washroom floor with your toothbrush and then use it to clean your teeth, or clean your teeth with a toothbrush someone else has used in their mouth?

/1
Laugh Point

Pass the book to Player 2 !... →

Player 2

(DON'T FORGET TO EXPLAIN YOUR ANSWERS!)

Would you rather eat your favourite food at every meal, or once a month?

/1 Laugh Point

Would you rather do a loud fart and have everyone know you did it, or a really stinky one and have nobody know?

/1 Laugh Point

Player 2

(DON'T FORGET TO EXPLAIN YOUR ANSWERS!)

Would you rather be a writer or a painter?

/1
Laugh Point

Would you rather eat food that tastes good but looks like poop or food that looks good but tastes like poop?

/1
Laugh Point

Player 1 /4
ROUD TOTAL

Player 2 /4
ROUD TOTAL

ROUD WINNER

Player

(DON'T FORGET TO EXPLAIN YOUR ANSWERS!)

Would you rather wear see-through clothes, or have everyone you know wear see-through clothes?

/1
Laugh Point

Would you rather never pick your nose but have people think you did or have to pick your nose and eat it every day, but have nobody know?

/1
Laugh Point

Player

(DON'T FORGET TO EXPLAIN YOUR ANSWERS!)

Would you rather step on dog poop while wearing shoes but not wash it off all day, or stand on dog poop in bare feet but wash it off immediately?

/1
Laugh Point

Would you rather shout all of the time or whisper?

/1
Laugh Point

Pass the book to Player 2 !... →

Player 2

(DON'T FORGET TO EXPLAIN YOUR ANSWERS!)

Would you rather eat a dead bug that tastes gross or a live bug that tastes good?

/1 Laugh Point

Would you rather eat asparagus flavored ice cream or ice cream flavored asparagus?

/1 Laugh Point

Player 2

(DON'T FORGET TO EXPLAIN YOUR ANSWERS!)

Would you rather have eyes that fire laser beams or freeze rays?

/1
Laugh Point

Would you rather change diapers all day for one week or clean a cat's litter tray every day for a year?

/1
Laugh Point

Player 1   /4
ROUD TOTAL

Player 2   /4
ROUD TOTAL

ROUD WINNER

Player 1

(DON'T FORGET TO EXPLAIN YOUR ANSWERS!)

Would you rather throw up every time you ate your favorite food, or never eat your favorite food again and never throw up?

/1
Laugh Point

Would you rather have smelly breath or smelly feet?

/1
Laugh Point

Player

(DON'T FORGET TO EXPLAIN YOUR ANSWERS!)

Would you rather eat cake every day or chips?

/1
Laugh Point

Would you rather use shampoo to brush your teeth or toothpaste to wash your hair?

/1
Laugh Point

Pass the book to Player 2 !... →

Player 2

(DON'T FORGET TO EXPLAIN YOUR ANSWERS!)

Would you rather swim through a pool of eels or a pool of jellyfish?

/1
Laugh Point

Would you rather be a cat or a dog?

/1
Laugh Point

Player

(DON'T FORGET TO EXPLAIN YOUR ANSWERS!)

Would you rather eat cereal out of your friend's mouth or have them eat cereal out of yours?

/1
Laugh Point

Would you rather fart clouds of sweet-smelling glitter or belch dusty clouds that smell like candy

/1
Laugh Point

Player 1 /4
ROUD TOTAL

Player 2 /4
ROUD TOTAL

ROUD WINNER

Player

(DON'T FORGET TO EXPLAIN YOUR ANSWERS!)

Would you rather never be able to tell a lie or never be able, to tell the truth?

/1
Laugh Point

Would you rather lose your sight and have super sensitive hearing or lose your hearing and have super sensitive eyesight?

/1
Laugh Point

Player 1

(DON'T FORGET TO EXPLAIN YOUR ANSWERS!)

Would you rather eat a worm or lick a slug?

/1
Laugh Point

Have super fart powers that make you fly or super burp powers that blow objects and people away?

/1
Laugh Point

Pass the book to Player 2 !... →

Player 2

(DON'T FORGET TO EXPLAIN YOUR ANSWERS!)

Poop in a dirty, smelly public toilet or poop behind the bushes at a park?

/1
Laugh Point

Burp the alphabet at a party or make fart noises to everyone's favorite song?

/1
Laugh Point

Player 2

(DON'T FORGET TO EXPLAIN YOUR ANSWERS!)

You have exclusive access to a time machine. Would you rather go 100 years back in the past or fast forward 100 years to the future?

/1 Laugh Point

Would you rather live outside in a tent or live inside and never be able to leave the house?

/1 Laugh Point

Player 1 /4
ROUD TOTAL

Player 2 /4
ROUD TOTAL

ROUD WINNER

Player 1

(DON'T FORGET TO EXPLAIN YOUR ANSWERS!)

Would you rather live underwater or in outer space?

/1
Laugh Point

Would you rather clean your nose out with your tongue OR have taste buds on your fingers and you taste everything you touch?

/1
Laugh Point

Player 1

(DON'T FORGET TO EXPLAIN YOUR ANSWERS!)

Would you rather use mucky tree sap as a lotion OR wet poison ivy leaves as wipes?

/1 Laugh Point

Would you rather ride a bike with ladybugs as wheels OR with lizards as the handles?

/1 Laugh Point

Pass the book to Player 2 !... →

Player 2

(DON'T FORGET TO EXPLAIN YOUR ANSWERS!)

Would you rather have your ear cleaned out with a giraffe's tongue OR praying mantis claws?

/1
Laugh Point

Would you rather be able to swing from buildings with your armpit hair OR fly with huge eyelashes?

/1
Laugh Point

Player 2

(DON'T FORGET TO EXPLAIN YOUR ANSWERS!)

Would you rather shoot glue out of your hand OR make it rain spit?

/1
Laugh Point

Would you rather have the mouth of a mole OR a squid?

/1
Laugh Point

Player 1 /4
ROUD TOTAL

Player 2 /4
ROUD TOTAL

ROUD WINNER

Player 1

(DON'T FORGET TO EXPLAIN YOUR ANSWERS!)

Would you rather suck out an eyeball with a straw OR your grandpa's fresh armpit sweat?

/1
Laugh Point

Would you rather brush with toilet water OR use it for cereal?

/1
Laugh Point

Player 1

(DON'T FORGET TO EXPLAIN YOUR ANSWERS!)

Would you rather be stuck on a planet of dirty dogs OR a planet of dirty cats?

/1
Laugh Point

Would you rather be in solitary confinement for 5 years or constantly in the presence of someone else for 5 years?

/1
Laugh Point

Pass the book to Player 2 !... →

Player 2

(DON'T FORGET TO EXPLAIN YOUR ANSWERS!)

Would you rather the stars be absent from the night sky or live with perpetual clouds during the daytime?

/1
Laugh Point

Would you rather live in a house without power or in a house without tap water?

/1
Laugh Point

Player 2

(DON'T FORGET TO EXPLAIN YOUR ANSWERS!)

If you are stranded on a deserted island, would you rather be stranded with someone you really don't like or on the island completely isolated?

/1
Laugh Point

Would you rather the stars be absent from the night sky or live with perpetual clouds during the daytime?

/1
Laugh Point

Player 1 /4
ROUD TOTAL

Player 2 /4
ROUD TOTAL

ROUD WINNER

Player

(DON'T FORGET TO EXPLAIN YOUR ANSWERS!)

Would you rather not be allowed to wash your hands for a month or your hair for a month?

/1
Laugh Point

Would you rather have to use a public toilet that is extremely dirty and dark or one that has a snake in it?

/1
Laugh Point

Player

(DON'T FORGET TO EXPLAIN YOUR ANSWERS!)

Would you rather risk going to the bathroom in an extremely gross/dirty public toilet in the dark or use a bathroom that has a sewer rat somewhere in it?

/1
Laugh Point

Would you rather share a toothbrush with your dog or a scrub brush with an outdoor pig?

/1
Laugh Point

Pass the book to Player 2 !... →

Player 2

(DON'T FORGET TO EXPLAIN YOUR ANSWERS!)

Would you rather have a permanently clogged nose or a piece of green food always stuck in your teeth?

/1
Laugh Point

Being completely barefoot, would you rather walk through a public bathroom or in poison ivy?

/1
Laugh Point

Player 2

(DON'T FORGET TO EXPLAIN YOUR ANSWERS!)

Would you rather lick a homeless man's toe or chew a piece of gum you found sticking to the underside of a table?

/1
Laugh Point

Would you rather pull your own thumbnail off with a fork or put a toothpick under your big toe and kick a wall?

/1
Laugh Point

Player  /4
ROUD TOTAL

Player 2 /4
ROUD TOTAL

ROUD WINNER

Add up all your points from each round.
The PLAYER with the most points is crowned
The Laugh Champion!

In the event of a tie, continue to the Round 16 for the tie-breaker round

Player 1 ___/4
GRAND TOTAL

Player 2 ___/4
GRAND TOTAL

_____
the laugh Champion

Player 1

(DON'T FORGET TO EXPLAIN YOUR ANSWERS!)

Would you rather puke up slimy slugs or have bricks come out every time you pooped?

/1
Laugh Point

Would you rather eat only insects for the rest of your life and live as you are now or eat normally and have constant diarrhea?

/1
Laugh Point

Player

(DON'T FORGET TO EXPLAIN YOUR ANSWERS!)

Would you rather eat only insects for the rest of your life and live as you are now OR eat normally and have constant diarrhea?

/1 Laugh Point

Would you rather have a cold sore that never ever goes away or poop your pants once a week for the rest of your life?

/1 Laugh Point

Pass the book to Player 2 !... →

Player 2

(DON'T FORGET TO EXPLAIN YOUR ANSWERS!)

Would you rather have diarrhea during your wedding ceremony or have it during your wedding night?

/1
Laugh Point

Would you rather drink up vomit from a dark alley ground or puke in your mouth every time someone said your name?

/1
Laugh Point

Player 2

(DON'T FORGET TO EXPLAIN YOUR ANSWERS!)

Would you rather be inside a porta-potty when it falls over or smell like dog poop during a super important interview?

/1 Laugh Point

Would you rather suck on a used tampon for a minute or make out with a public toilet seat for a minute?

/1 Laugh Point

Pass the book to Player 1 !... →

Player 1

(DON'T FORGET TO EXPLAIN YOUR ANSWERS!)

Would you rather eat a whole raw chicken or drink a coffee cup full of liquefied slugs?

/1
Laugh Point

Would you rather drink a gallon of someone else's armpit sweat or drink a gallon of your own toe sweat?

/1
Laugh Point

Player 1

(DON'T FORGET TO EXPLAIN YOUR ANSWERS!)

Would you rather wear a trash bag with wet mold inside or sunbathe on a trash can lid filled with maggots?

/1 Laugh Point

Would you rather be a dinosaur teeth cleaner or help ants shower?

/1 Laugh Point

Pass the book to Player 2 !... →

Player 2

(DON'T FORGET TO EXPLAIN YOUR ANSWERS!)

Would you rather have shower tip toeing in a plate or fill tub with water using a teaspoon?

/1
Laugh Point

Would you let snails crawl in your ear or slugs crawl over your mouth?

/1
Laugh Point

Player 2

(DON'T FORGET TO EXPLAIN YOUR ANSWERS!)

Would you rather travel in a watermelon cat car or a kiwi fruit dog?

/1
Laugh Point

Would you rather get worn like a coat or a shoe?

/1
Laugh Point

Add up all your points from Round 11. The PLAYER with the most points is crowned The Laugh Champion

Player 1 ___/8
ROUD TOTAL

Player 2 ___/8
ROUD TOTAL

the laugh Champion

Manufactured by Amazon.ca
Bolton, ON

36893133R00059